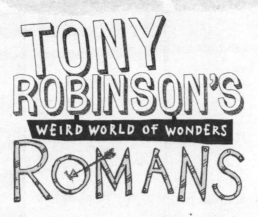

TONY ROBINSON'S
WEIRD WORLD OF WONDERS
ROMANS

Tony Robinson has written lots of books about history and ancient stuff, including *Tony Robinson's Kings and Queens* and *The Worst Children's Jobs in History*, which won the Best Book with Facts category of the Blue Peter Book Awards 2007. He has also written several television series for children, including *Maid Marian and Her Merry Men*, for which he received a BAFTA and a Royal Television Society Award. He presents Channel 4's archaeology series *Time Team* and played Baldrick in *Blackadder*.

Del Thorpe has been drawing ever since that time he ruined his mum's best tablecloth with wax crayons. Most of his formative work can be found in the margins of his old school exercise books. His maths teacher described these misunderstood works as 'wasting time'. When he left normal school, Del went to art school and drew serious, grown-up things. Soon he decided the ▯▯▯▯ ▯p stuff was mostly ▯▯▯▯▯▯▯▯▯▯▯▯▯▯▯▯▯▯ nd silly carto

Other books by Tony Robinson

TONY ROBINSON'S

WEIRD WORLD OF WONDERS

ROMANS

Illustrated by Del Thorpe

MACMILLAN CHILDREN'S BOOKS

For Holly . . .

This book is for Holly Shepherd-Robinson. She's only two years old, so she can't read it yet. But she can nibble at it, wear it as a hat, or drop it from a great height so it goes *bang!* on the floor.

Hopefully in about five years' time she'll try to read it. But by then it'll be so dog-eared and manky and stained with tomato ketchup that she'll have to buy her own copy, and I'll make about 17p!

. . . and Jess

It's also for Jessica Cobb, whose brains are bigger than a double-decker bus. In fact, if she didn't stick her head out of the window when she's on the way home, she'd squash all the other passengers. I couldn't have written the book without her.

First published 2012 by Macmillan Children's Books
a division of Macmillan Publishers Limited
20 New Wharf Road, London N1 9RR
Basingstoke and Oxford
Associated companies throughout the world
www.panmacmillan.com

ISBN 978-0-330-53389-8

Text copyright © Tony Robinson 2012
Illustrations copyright © Del Thorpe 2012

The right of Tony Robinson and Del Thorpe to be identified as the
author and illustrator of this work has been asserted by them in accordance
with the Copyright, Designs and Patents Act 1988.

1 3 5 7 9 8 6 4 2

A CIP catalogue record for this book is available from
the British Library.

Typeset by Dan Newman/Perfect Bound Ltd
Printed and bound by CPI Group (UK) Ltd, Croydon CR0 4YY

Hi! We're the Curiosity Crew. You may spot us hanging about in this book, checking stuff out.

It's about the Roman Empire, which in ancient times ruled pretty much all the known world for hundreds of years. That's impressive, particularly when you think that Rome started off in about 750 BC as an ordinary little farming village.

Although, actually, there's a much better story about how the whole Roman thing began, and it's pretty wild . . . that's if you believe it!

Read on to find out . . .

Stig   Nits   Grace   Peewee   Jojo

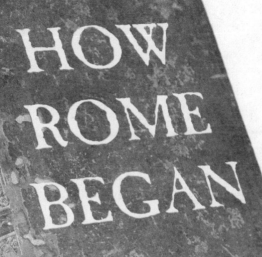

HOW ROME BEGAN

L ong, long ago in the faraway country of Italy there lived a beautiful young priestess called Rhea Silvia who began to grow fat. After six months she had a belly the size of a watermelon, and her uncle Amulius grabbed her by the sleeve, dragged her into the temple garden and whispered, 'You're pregnant!'

'That would seem to be the case,' replied Rhea Silvia.

'But you're a priestess. You're not allowed to mess around with young men,' insisted Amulius.

'I didn't,' said Rhea Silvia. 'I messed around with one of the gods – Mars. We went into those mulberry bushes, and one thing led to another, and now . . .'

'You're going to have a baby.'

'No,' said Rhea Silvia. 'I'm going to have two babies.'

And she did. Three months later Rhea Silvia gave birth to twins.

Her father King Numitor was naturally very upset, but he grew fond of the two little boys, and soon everyone was happy again . . .

Except Uncle Amulius.

One night he crept into the little boys' room, bundled them into a wicker basket and carried them off to the deep, dark forest.

'You have brought shame on our family,' he hissed. 'So now you must die.' And he tipped them out on to the musty, dusty leaves, leaving them to their fate.

All night they lay there. They didn't cry — they were brave little boys. But they were very hungry.

Then towards morning there was a snuffling sound, and the pad of soft paws, and a great, grey wolf loped out of the surrounding trees.

Mummy?

The wolf picked up one twin in her sharp, white teeth and carried him back to her den. Then she returned, picked up the other one, and brought him back to her den too.

But she didn't harm them. Her cubs had recently died in a tragic chariot accident, and she was full of milk and without any babies to love.

So she looked after the little boys and raised them as her own. She chased away the hungry badgers when they came too close to the den, and she covered them with the musty, dusty leaves when they were cold in winter. And they became strong and clever, and as wily as . . . err . . . wolves.

Stop! Stop this story right now!

Until one day, when they were eight years old, and their Wolf Mother had died and gone to Wolf Heaven, they were discovered by shepherds and taken back to the shepherds' village. There they were given a hut to live in, clothes to wear and names too. One was named Romulus and the other Remus.

This isn't true, you know.

By the time the boys had grown to manhood, Rhea Silvia's father was no longer king. Wicked Uncle Amulius had seized the crown, and had thrown Numitor into a damp and unhygienic dungeon. In fact Amulius threw almost anyone he could into that deep and unhygienic dungeon, and one day when Remus had strayed too near the palace while looking for a lost lamb, Amulius grabbed him and threw him in for trespassing.

The young man soon befriended Numitor, who told him his two grandsons had once been stolen from him. Fortunately Remus had an unusual birthmark behind his knee, and one afternoon Numitor saw it. He suddenly realised who Remus was — his long-lost grandson!

Unusual birthmark? This is getting more stupid by the minute!

Meanwhile Romulus had raised an army of brave shepherds who marched to the palace, broke down the door, seized Amulius, chopped him into bite-sized nuggets and threw him in the moat.

When the shepherds released Remus, he told them that he and his brother were heirs to the throne. The whole city cheered, held a three-day party and offered Romulus and Remus the crown. But they refused.

'Our grandfather Numitor is the rightful king,' they said. 'He shall rule here. We will set off and found a new city.'

So their mother Rhea Silvia brushed a tear from her eye, packed their lunch boxes and kissed them goodbye, and off they went, accompanied by the shepherds and a few scruffy, runaway slaves.

Ignore this, young reader! It's a pack of lies.

The Romans like to believe it, though!

After several days they came to two hills. One was called the Palatine Hill. 'We'll build our city here!' said Romulus.

The other was called the Aventine Hill. 'No, we'll build our city here,' said Remus.

And they began to argue. Romulus dug a trench and Remus filled it in again.

Remus lay some foundations, and Romulus walked all over the wet concrete in his big boots.

Romulus built a brick wall, and Remus kicked it over.

This was too much for Romulus. He picked up a rusty shovel, hit Remus on the head, and Remus fell down dead.

'We shall build my city here on the Palatine Hill,' announced Romulus. 'And what is more we will name it after me.

'It will be called Rome, and we shall be known as the Romans!'

Romans! Romans! Yeah, yeah, we're the Romans!

But there was a small problem . . .

'We're all men,' said the shepherds and the scruffy, runaway slaves. 'You can't start a city with ALL men.'

'Then I'll fetch some women,' Romulus replied, and straight away, he marched down into the valley and captured all the women who lived there. He brought them back to Rome and made them become Roman wives, even though some of them were extremely annoyed.

From above, Mars looked down on his son's city and he loved it. He would make it the most powerful place in the land . . . and that's how Rome began.

No, it's not! Rome was NOT founded by a badly behaved boy who'd been brought up by a wolf, but by a sophisticated people called the Etruscans. They taught the Romans mathematics, architecture and loads of other stuff. Even the word 'Roman' is an Etruscan word.

11

THE SONS OF MARS

PART ONE

By 300 BC, the city of Rome had built up a powerful army. Roman men reckoned they were as good at fighting as Romulus's dad, Mars the god of war, so they called themselves 'The Sons of Mars'. They were **incredibly** proud of their army – and you can't blame them. It was a lean, mean fighting machine.

If it had been a football team, it would have been Chelsea, Man U and Barcelona combined. It would have won the League, the Cup and Champions League not just once, but for **centuries**.

Roman centurions, who were top army officers, wore these fancy helmets.

INSULTS ACROSS THE SEA

So Rome went to war and once it had taken over all the little kingdoms around it . . .

Including the land of the Etruscans!

. . . it started eyeing up massive places further afield.

One of the most powerful was **Carthage** – a city on the North African coast, just across the other side of the Mediterranean Sea. Rome hated Carthage and Carthage hated Rome, but for a long time neither was strong enough to crush the other. So they just sort of glared at one another and shouted insults.

CRAZY HANNIBAL

Then a new young general took command of Carthage's army. His name was Hannibal and he wasn't going to take any more Roman aggravation. He decided not just to attack Rome, but to **invade** it.

But rather than popping across to Italy in a few boats, he sailed to Spain. Then he marched his army through Spain, across France and over the Alps, the big mountains that divide France and Italy!

This came as a bit of a shock to the Romans – who didn't expect anyone to be **crazy** enough to climb over a massive range of snow-covered mountains to get at them.

But that's exactly why Hannibal did it . . . not because he was crazy (OK, well maybe a bit) but because he knew the Romans wouldn't be expecting it!

Here Hannibal is holding the Roman standard (a stick with a big symbol at the end). He's turned it upside down, to show he beat the Romans.

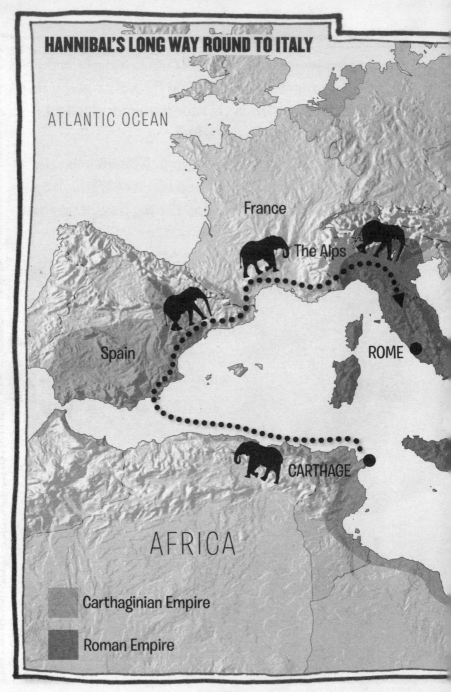

HANNIBAL'S LONG WAY ROUND TO ITALY

ATLANTIC OCEAN

France

The Alps

Spain

ROME

CARTHAGE

AFRICA

Carthaginian Empire

Roman Empire

WAR ELEPHANTS

The army Hannibal took with him over the Alps included more than 30 **elephants**.

This may seem a bit weird, but ancient armies were quite keen on using elephants in battle. There's nothing like hundreds of angry jumbos charging at the enemy to make them think twice!

But however impressive they were, Hannibal's elephants weren't much use to him. Most of them died on their way through the mountains and the ones which didn't were pretty knackered . . . but then so would you be if you'd just walked all the way from Africa.

The Romans decided to send a vast army of 80,000 soldiers to face Hannibal at Cannae in south-east Italy.

Unfortunately for Rome, Hannibal was very good at coming up with sneaky and surprising ways to win. He'd already won a battle at sea by throwing barrels of poisonous snakes into the enemy boats. That's the kind of commander he was – you had to watch him because you never knew what he was going to do next!

Realizing he was outnumbered, Hannibal made sure that when the Romans advanced, his army deliberately gave way. The Romans charged forward and the edges of Hannibal's army closed around them in a big circle.

The Roman army was trapped and Hannibal's troops attacked them from all sides. More than 50,000 Roman soldiers are said to have been slaughtered – one writer said that the Carthaginians killed them at the rate of 600 men a minute until night fell.

BATTLE OF CANNAE

Date: 216 BC

Roman Army: 80,000

Carthaginians: 50,000 (including a handful of very tired elephants)

Score: 10-nil to Carthage (or 'a draw' if you're a Roman)

Man of the match: Super-striker Hannibal

Cannae was a big defeat for the Romans, like being relegated from the Premier League or losing in the first round of the cup.

Anyone else would have blamed the ref, or gone home to have a bit of a cry . . . but not the Romans.

No – they absolutely refused to accept that they were beaten. The way they saw it – if the city of Rome was still standing, then they **hadn't** been defeated!

On the one hand this is a bit mental, but on the other hand it explains why it was so difficult to defeat the Romans. Unless you marched into the city of Rome itself, set fire to it, crushed all the buildings into little bits and stomped up and down on the blackened

Let's go home, Jumbo.

Sure thing, Dumbo.

remains, there were always going to be Romans shouting *'Come on, chaps! We're not beaten yet!'*

And sure enough, within a year the Romans had got a new army together, and headed for Carthage. Hannibal was forced to leave Italy to defend his homeland.

Once again he decided to rely on war elephants. But this time, the Romans were ready for him – when the elephants charged, the Roman soldiers blew loud horns, causing them to panic and trample on their own troops. The Roman army encircled Hannibal's army and **destroyed** it. Rome may have lost the Battle of Cannae, but it won the war!

Losers! Losers!

NASTY NOISES AND STINKY SMELLS

Most people in ancient times lived in little villages. The biggest excitement they got in a day was if someone fell over in the mud, or if a pig got the hiccups! But not in Rome . . .

Thanks to the success of its army, Rome was soon the largest city in the world and home to over one million people – a sprawling mass of houses, temples, theatres, baths and shops.

If you were a visitor from one of those tiny villages, your jaw would have practically hit the pavement at the sheer size and magnificence of the place!

HANDS OVER YOUR EARS

It was jam-packed. Most Romans lived crowded together in apartment blocks divided by narrow streets full of traffic and people.

And it was incredibly noisy. There were the
piercing shouts of street sellers, the racket
of wooden carts, the plink and plonk of
musicians, knife grinders setting your teeth on
edge, and the bashing and crashing of carpenters and
metalsmiths.

SHAPES IN THE ASH

The ancient city of Pompeii in southern Italy tells us loads about what Roman houses looked like, what type of work Romans did and what they ate.

On 24 August 79 AD, a volcano called Mount Vesuvius erupted and buried Pompeii in hot ash and lava. Houses, people and animals were covered in the ash, which cooled and hardened like rock.

1,700 years later, the city was rediscovered and dug out. Everything looked like it did the day the volcano erupted. Bread was still in the ovens, food in the restaurants, tools in the workshops and furniture in the houses.

There was even ancient graffiti written on some of the walls, and it was the same type of stuff people write today like:

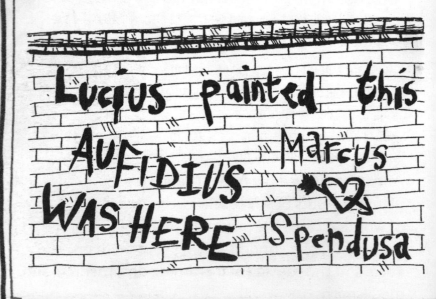

People caught fleeing from the eruption, frozen in time.

Bodies had decomposed but left shapes in the hardened ash. Experts filled these holes with plaster to create statues of the people and animals killed in the disaster.

There are still lots more things to find in Pompeii. The only problem is that digging it up might destroy it. Some people are worried that the buildings are starting to crumble and break. Plus, lots of tourists visit Pompeii and walk all over it chipping off bits to take home as souvenirs!

A plaster cast of a man trying to protect his eyes from the ash.

HANDS OVER YOUR MOUTHS

Apart from the noise, another massive problem was the smell. With so many people living and working close together, the streets quickly filled with rubbish, rotting food and lots of poo.

Luckily, the Romans had a system to wash it away!

Think of all the reasons you need water – drinking, cooking, cleaning, washing ... that's a lot of wet stuff, isn't it? But times it by a million and that's how much water Rome needed every day. Unfortunately, people couldn't use the water from the local

How to build an aqueduct.

Phew!

Ack

river because it got really dirty and they'd have found themselves guzzling dishwater and other people's wee.

So the Romans built 'aqueducts' – long channels for bringing in fresh water from springs outside the city. Being Romans, they didn't mess around if there was a problem. When there was a valley in the way, they just built a bridge with a channel inside it to carry the water.

At one time Rome had nine aqueducts delivering 46 million gallons of water to the city every day. It collected in big reservoirs, then flowed through pipes into fountains, baths and private villas all round the city. Once it had been used, the dirty water from the streets, houses and toilets flowed back out of the city in sewer pipes.

MAKING THE RULES – PART ONE

Building things like sewers and public toilets was very complicated, and the Romans needed a strong government to persuade people to cough up the money for all that digging and plumbing. But they were fed up with having kings like Romulus telling them what to do; it was their money, and they wanted to be able to decide how to spend it. So they turned their city into a 'Republic', which basically means they ran it themselves.

In charge was the Senate, 300 posh people who claimed they were related to the very earliest Roman shepherds . . .

HANDS OVER YOUR NOSES

Many Romans didn't have their own loo, but you could pay a small fee to use a public toilet, where you sat on a bench and did your business through a hole into a channel below. It wasn't very private – you just sat between lots of other people doing the same thing, and when you wanted to wipe your bum someone passed you a sponge on a stick!

Roman toilets could sit up to 60 people – yikes!

MAKING THE RULES – PART TWO

The Roman Republic was really successful – all Roman citizens felt they had a say in how Rome was run and were really proud of it. And to remind everyone of that fact, the letters **SPQR** (which stood for **'Senatus Populus Que Romanus'** or **'The Senate and People of Rome'**) were stamped not only on Roman coins, but on Roman buildings, Roman paving stones and even Roman drainpipes!

A Roman mosaic – it's that wolf and the twins again.

I'm certainly proud to be a Roman.

So am I. I've even had a reminder stamped on my head!

SPQR

The poor didn't have enough money to go to public toilets, so they used a pot instead. When it was full, they were supposed to take it out and empty it into a sewer, but lots of people couldn't be bothered ... and chucked the contents out of the window on to the streets below!

Run for it!

GET YOUR WHITES WHITE ...

Not all Rome's wee went down a sewer or over people's heads. Ever wondered how the Romans kept their togas so white?

They sent them off to the fuller's shop to be washed, dyed, rinsed and dried. The chemicals in human urine are very good for cleaning cloth, so the fullers soaked people's clothes in vats of pee, which they bought from the city's public toilets!

The Roman Baths in Bath, which is named after the baths.

A NICE LONG SOAK

Romans were big fans of baths and bathing. There was nothing they liked more than taking a long soak in a hot bath and having a good scrub. But not many people could afford their own bath.

So big public baths were built for everyone to use. These were a bit like a health club – they had pools, hot tubs, saunas, steam rooms and gyms. There were places to get a massage or a haircut, quiet corners where you could read, and there were even people selling fast food if you felt a bit peckish.

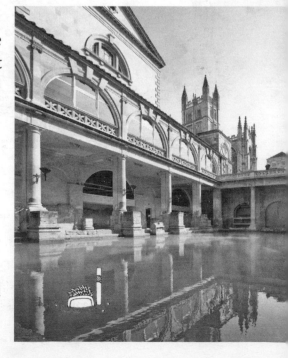

Inside, you could have a cold bath (a *'frigidarium'*), a warm bath (a *'tepidarium'*) and a hot bath (a *'caldarium'*) with water heated by a furnace. Often you would use all of them, one after the other!

You didn't use soap – instead you rubbed your skin with oil and cleaned it off with a metal scraper. This took off all the dirt, dead skin and sweat. If you were rich, your slaves would do it for you. And no one wanted to be hairy. So you hired someone to pluck out your body hair with a pair of tweezers!

There were hundreds of baths in Rome, and they were usually packed. People went there to hang out with their friends, have business meetings or just chill out.

THE SONS OF MARS

PART TWO

When Rome was just a medium-sized city, its army was made up of ordinary farmers who bought a shield and helmet, then took time off work to march around being soldiers for a bit. But once Rome got really big this became a serious problem. It was all very well asking farmers to leave their work to fight the odd battle, but war was becoming a full-time occupation.

The farmers needed to be doing other things like mucking out their cows, sowing their seeds and pulling up their turnips. They couldn't just go off gallivanting around the world all the time, bashing foreigners.

So Rome started to pay people to fight. Then, once they had a decent wage, a shiny new kit and three hot meals a day, Roman soldiers happily spent years travelling the world beating people up to their hearts' content!

DO THE MATHS

The Roman army was divided into **legions** of about 5,000 men. Start counting!

Each legion was divided into ten **cohorts** (480 men).

Each cohort was made up of six **centuries** (80 men).

And every century was split into ten teams of eight men who shared a tent. (After sharing a tent with seven sweaty soldiers you probably looked forward to a good battle, if only to get some fresh air.)

TATTS AND TAGS

Soldiers signed up for 25 years. In ancient times you were lucky to live past 40, so this was pretty much signing up for life!

You didn't have to be from Rome to be a soldier – they came from all the places the Romans had invaded. Lots of the soldiers who served in Britain were from North Africa.

If you wanted to join up, you had to be a free man (no women or slaves were allowed), at least 5 feet 10 inches tall and aged 20–25 years old. But some units weren't that picky, and if you were big for your age you might get in at 14 or 15.

After joining you received a lead identity tag to hang round your neck, and sometimes you also got a tattoo on your hand, so that the army could identify you if you changed your mind and tried to run away.

Soldiers still wear identity tags around their necks today.

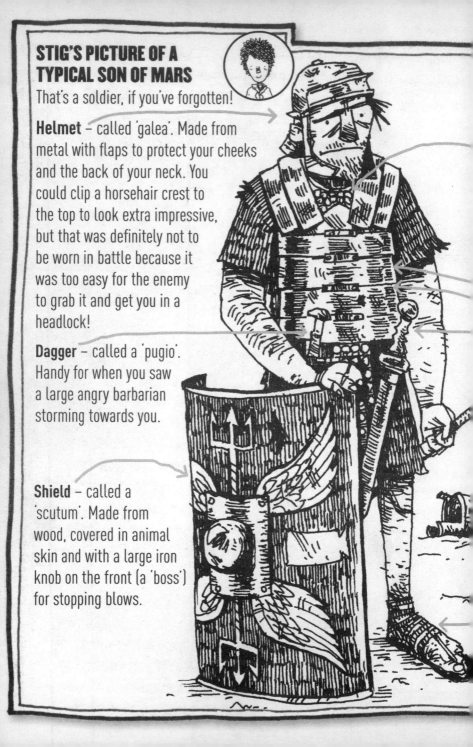

STIG'S PICTURE OF A TYPICAL SON OF MARS

That's a soldier, if you've forgotten!

Helmet – called 'galea'. Made from metal with flaps to protect your cheeks and the back of your neck. You could clip a horsehair crest to the top to look extra impressive, but that was definitely not to be worn in battle because it was too easy for the enemy to grab it and get you in a headlock!

Dagger – called a 'pugio'. Handy for when you saw a large angry barbarian storming towards you.

Shield – called a 'scutum'. Made from wood, covered in animal skin and with a large iron knob on the front (a 'boss') for stopping blows.

Big stick – called a 'pilum', with a metal point on the end. Could be thrown up to 100 feet. If it didn't kill the enemy, he'd spend the rest of the battle trying to get this lethal weapon out of his shield.

Mail armour – made of lots of metal links joined together to make a sort of heavy metal jumper.

Another sort of armour – called 'lorica segmentata'. Made of overlapping strips of metal attached to leather straps.

Padding – under the armour. Because metal armour might save your life but it was really uncomfortable!

Sword – called a 'gladius'. It was double-edged, which meant you could just wave it about and be sure to do a bit of damage somewhere.

Boots – called 'caligas'. These were sandals with metal studs in the bottom for added grip (also good for stomping on the enemy, but not for chasing him across a marble floor, as you would probably skid, fall over and stab yourself).

COWS FOR TARGET PRACTICE

If you were a new recruit in the army, you had to train every day.

You're probably thinking – hey, being trained to fight doesn't sound so bad; learning how to kick ass . . . I could do that.

Well, it's true that Roman soldiers learned to fight; they practised with heavy wooden swords and shields, fought mock battles and even used the heads of dead cows as target practice. Yes, really.

But this was only part of their training. They were also taught another important skill . . . the art of walking a long way while carrying lots of heavy things.

The Roman army was on the go from dawn to dusk, marching from place to place and pitching their tents at the end of each day. And when they weren't marching or fighting, the soldiers were building things like roads and forts.

So they were specially trained to march 18 miles in five hours in full armour while carrying all their kit – including their weapons, shield, food, spare clothes, a short spade, a tool kit, a cooking pot, a big stone for grinding corn and two wooden stakes (in case they needed to put up a protective fence round their camp).

The whole lot weighed about 30 kilograms – that's the same weight as an average eight-year-old. So if you're eight, you could tell your friends that you're as heavy as a Roman soldier's backpack. Then you could get them to see if they're tough enough to carry you 18 miles. My bet is most of them would collapse after 18 metres!

To make sure the recruits were good at walking and carrying, they were made to practise **a lot**. And a burly bloke with a big stick marched behind them to whack anyone who wanted to go home early.

In fact you got whacked for virtually everything you did wrong, except for really serious crimes which were punished by death. Soldiers who ran away in battle were crucified (nailed to a wooden cross and left to die) or were thrown to wild animals, while soldiers who went to sleep while on

Soldiers, from the left – number . . .

One!

Two!

Three!

Four!

Five!

guard were clubbed to death by their comrades for putting everyone's lives at risk.

If a whole unit fled from a battle they were '**decimated**'. 'Decimation' means 'removal of a tenth'. In other words, one in every ten soldiers was picked out and slaughtered!

Nevertheless, running away from the Roman army was pretty common, even though you risked such a terrible fate if you did it.

GROSS MOUSTACHES

But all the practice and ferocious discipline paid off. The Roman army marched all over Europe and successfully conquered tribe after tribe, and country after country.

One of its most successful generals was Julius Caesar. He was given the job of defeating the Gauls of northern France. The Romans called this area 'Gallia Comata', which means **Hairy Gaul** – because the tribes who lived there wore their hair long and had big moustaches.

The Romans couldn't stand moustaches. They thought they were unhygienic. They said that when the Gauls ate their meat, half of it got stuck and dangled in their face-hair, and when they drank, the booze ran through it like a sieve!

The tribes of Gaul had united under one leader called Vercingetorix. Gauls had crazy names to match their crazy moustaches.

Caesar's army pursued Vercingetorix and his men all over Gaul and eventually cornered them at a place called Alesia. The Gauls were inside Alesia looking out, and the Romans were outside looking in.

Caesar decided to wait the Gauls out – he figured it was only a matter of time before they ran out of food and were forced to eat their own moustaches. In the meantime, to be sure no more supplies got in and to keep his soldiers busy, he ordered a **huge wooden wall** be built around the town. The wall had . . .

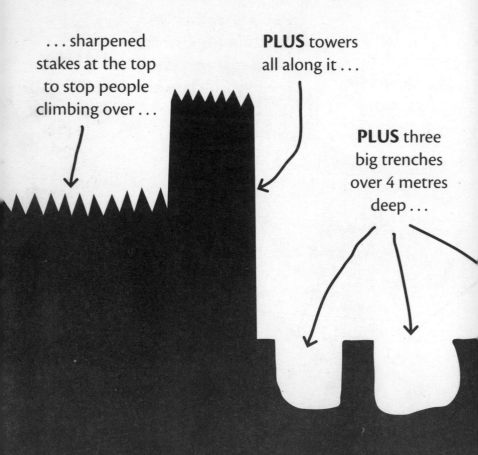

. . . sharpened stakes at the top to stop people climbing over . . .

PLUS towers all along it . . .

PLUS three big trenches over 4 metres deep . . .

Caesar's soldiers were **so** brilliant at lifting, carrying and building that within a few weeks the wall was 10 miles long and 4 metres high.

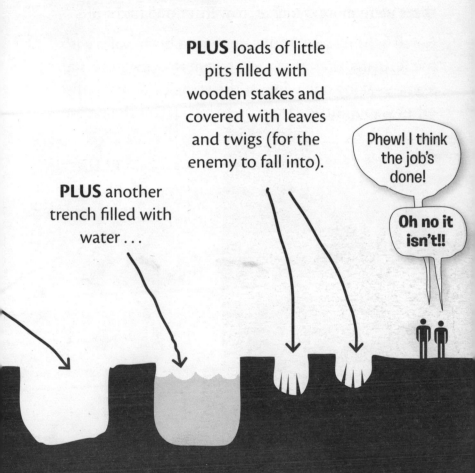

PLUS loads of little pits filled with wooden stakes and covered with leaves and twigs (for the enemy to fall into).

PLUS another trench filled with water . . .

Phew! I think the job's done!

Oh no it isn't!!

Then Caesar heard that 100,000 more Gauls were on their way to help rescue Vercingetorix's men. So he ordered his army to build **another** wall to protect them from the approaching Gauls. This second wall was even longer, running 14 miles round his men . . . **PLUS** there were more trenches, towers and loads of pits.

Fierce fighting soon broke out along both walls, with the Romans attempting to prevent Vercingetorix's army from breaking out, while at the same time stopping the other Gauls outside from breaking in. Get the picture?

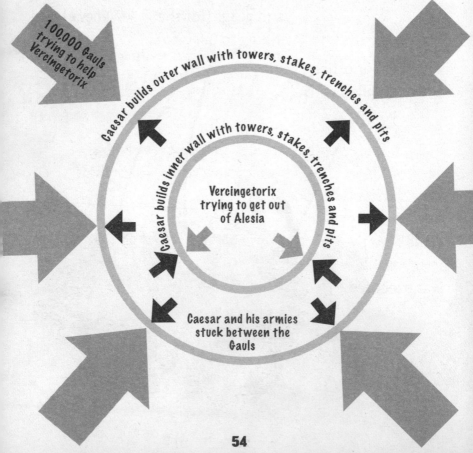

100,000 Gauls trying to help Vercingetorix

Caesar builds outer wall with towers, stakes, trenches and pits

Caesar builds inner wall with towers, stakes, trenches and pits

Vercingetorix trying to get out of Alesia

Caesar and his armies stuck between the Gauls

Despite being outnumbered 3 to 1, the Roman army defeated the attacking Gauls and prevented them from rescuing Vercingetorix's army. Vercingetorix and his men were forced to surrender or face starvation. The Gauls were beaten.

SIEGE OF ALESIA

Date: 52 BC

Roman Army: 60,000

Gauls: 80,000 inside the fort, plus another 100,000 outside!

Score: Romans –2, Gauls – 0

Man of the Match: Julius Caesar.

Vercingetorix was taken back to Rome in chains and was kept in prison for five years before being paraded through the streets as part of a big celebration of Caesar's military victories. After that, just to show everyone that no one should mess with the Romans, he was executed.

PEEWEE'S LIST OF ROMAN WEAPONS

The Roman army had some pretty nasty machines to help it fight people hidden behind giant walls. These included:

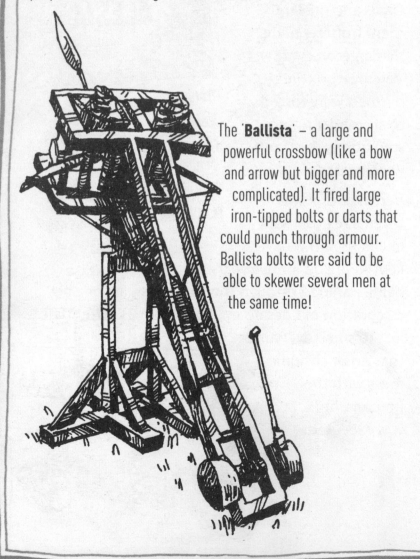

The '**Ballista**' – a large and powerful crossbow (like a bow and arrow but bigger and more complicated). It fired large iron-tipped bolts or darts that could punch through armour. Ballista bolts were said to be able to skewer several men at the same time!

The '**Onager**' – a giant catapult, which could be wound up and then released to fling massive chunks of rock at walls. 'Onager' means 'wild ass' because it kicked like a donkey!

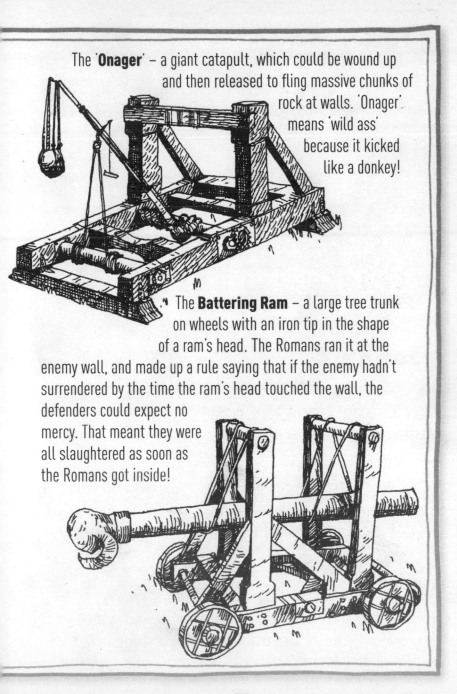

The **Battering Ram** – a large tree trunk on wheels with an iron tip in the shape of a ram's head. The Romans ran it at the enemy wall, and made up a rule saying that if the enemy hadn't surrendered by the time the ram's head touched the wall, the defenders could expect no mercy. That meant they were all slaughtered as soon as the Romans got inside!

POOR KIDS RICH KIDS

POOR KIDS

Poor kids in ancient Rome lived in little flats and ate pizza. Rich ones spent all their time learning Latin and feasting on peacock's brains. Which would you rather have been?

Either way, you had to keep pretty quiet and do what you were told. Any kid who complained risked getting beaten, chucked out of the house or sold into slavery!

ROTTEN DADS

In ancient Rome, dads ruled. I mean they **really** ruled – they were the head of the family and not only owned your house but every single thing in it ... including you! You literally belonged to your dad, and

he was allowed to do whatever he wanted with you. When a baby was born, it was laid at its father's feet – if he picked it up it became part of the family, but if he didn't, it was abandoned.

Today if you misbehave, about the worst thing most parents will do to you is send you to your room. But in ancient Rome if you drove your dad nuts, he could take you miles away from home and abandon you in the street, or sell you as a slave to somebody else!

Until the first century AD, a father was even allowed to kill his children if he wanted!

Someone liked this lad enough to carve his face. He did grow up to be Emperor Nero, mind.

I'm highly educated, you know.

It wouldn't have mattered if your mum wanted to keep you – mums didn't have much say in ancient Rome. They were expected to run the home, keep everything tidy, raise the children, cook nice food . . . and that was it.

Women belonged to their dad or their husband. For a long time they weren't even allowed to own things (everything in the house belonged to the head of the family), and they couldn't vote for changes to the law – so they just had to put up with things as they were, although I bet they worked out how to get their way when they wanted to!

DO I HAVE TO GO TO SCHOOL?

Lots of kids in ancient Rome didn't go to school – they were taught at home instead. Girls learned how to clean, sew and cook, while boys were taught whatever skills their dad thought they needed.

Lesson One:
Always obey your father.
Lesson Two:
Rome is great.
Lesson Three:
See Lesson One.

Most kids learned basic reading and writing and a bit of maths . . . but not for long – from the age of ten, boys started working and girls got ready to get married!!

If you were from a rich family you had more of an education – you were sent to school till you were sixteen, were taught how to read and write in Latin and Greek, and how to speak in public.

Paper was rare and really expensive, so you practised writing by getting a pointed stick and scratching words on tablets covered in wax. If you wanted to erase something, you just smeared the wax back over the tablet and started again.

Some kids messed about, sketching funny pictures of their teachers on the wax tablets, or scraping the wax off it to make models. The sharp sticks were also handy for scratching your name on other things . . . like walls.

If you were caught, the teacher would smack your hands with a cane, or whip your back with strips of leather.

Roman teachers who did this a lot were given nicknames like 'leather arm' and 'the whacker'!

Teachers weren't paid very much. In fact, one complained that he got paid in a year what a chariot driver got paid for one race!

A **chariot driver** would get glamour, excitement, money – and possibly an early death.

Hmm...

A **teacher** would get pesky kids, loads of homework to mark – and a long, pleasant retirement in a villa by the sea.

Which would you rather be?

A teacher?

Yeah – right!

WAYS WITH WORDS

The language the Romans used was called Latin . . . Hang on a moment – here is a newsflash!

We **interrupt** this **chapter** to bring you a **special announcement**. **Scientists** have **discovered aliens**. They are a **strange type** of **animal** with **six tentacles**, and they've **promised** not to **eat** us if we send them **flowers**. **Florists** are **expected** to sell out of **roses** soon, which are **apparently** their **favourite**.

This newsflash (actually it's not real, did you realize that?) shows how many of the words we use today come from Latin. All the **bold** words are Latin, the normal ones aren't.

Even the word 'language' comes from the Latin word '**lingua**' – which means tongue!

ECLASMARIVSVENANT
ASILIVSVCETINLPRA
RBPATRICIVSCONS
RDINARIVSARENAN
ODIVMQVÆABON
ANDITERRÆMO
VSRVINAPROS
RAVTSVITVPR
RIONESIIVI

Latin has letters that we still use today, which is handy. But the Romans didn't use J, U or W, and they didn't always bother putting spaces between words – so it looks like a load of nonsense!

THE CURIOSITY CREW TEACHES YOU TO SPEAK THE LINGO

Here are some Latin phrases to impress your friends . . .

Te audire non possum est. Musa sapientum fixa est in aure.

I can't hear you. I have a banana in my ear.

Non torsii subligarium!

Don't get your knickers in a twist!

. . . Unfortunately they probably won't understand you, because not many people speak Latin any more.

In dentibus acticis frustum magnum spiniciae habes.

You have a big piece of spinach in your teeth.

Catapultam habeo. Nisi pecuniam omnem mihi dabis, ad caput tuum saxum immanem mittam.

I have a catapult. Unless you give me all your money, I will fling an enormous rock at your head.

MOUSE AND CART

When they weren't busy learning Latin and doing whatever their dads told them to, Roman kids played with toys, games and pets.

Most of their toys sound a bit lame to us – things like balls, spinning tops, hoops, toy soldiers and dolls made of clay or wax.

But there are also descriptions of Roman kids fighting mock battles with wooden swords, and playing tug-of-war games where one team had to try and pull another team across a line.

This way . . .

Lots of children kept pet birds – doves, ducks, crows and geese were popular – and if you were lucky you might even own a pet monkey! Some kids had dogs which they hooked up to mini-chariots, then raced them round the streets. Others made little carts for mice to pull.

Who needs a Wii when you've got a mouse pulling a tiny cart!

AND NOW THE RICH KIDS

Rich kids lived in big villas. They had kitchens, dining rooms, baths, a garden and everyone had their own bedroom. You might even have had a villa near the city **and** a seaside home for the summer.

No, this way!

Aaaaagh!

JOJO'S GUIDE TO RICH KIDS' HOUSES

A rich kid's luxury villa was kitted out with ancient state-of-the-art technology . . .

Central heating: The Romans designed a way to keep their feet toasty warm, because their villas had stone floors which got chilly in winter. Spaces under the floor called hypocausts were filled with hot air heated by a furnace.

Glass windows: Glass was a new invention and mostly used for making small things like bottles and cups. But some rich Romans had little glass windows – although they couldn't see much through them because the glass was bluey-green with bubbles in it!

HEAT

Baths: Lots of villas had their own bath-houses with steam rooms (heated by the hypocaust) and ice-cold plunge baths.

Swanky decorations: The floors and walls were often decorated with mosaics – pictures made up of thousands of tiny pieces of coloured stone (even simple mosaics had around 100,000 pieces, some smaller than your fingernail). You could choose the picture you wanted from a book or design your own, then someone would come and fit it all together. A bit like doing the world's biggest jigsaw puzzle!

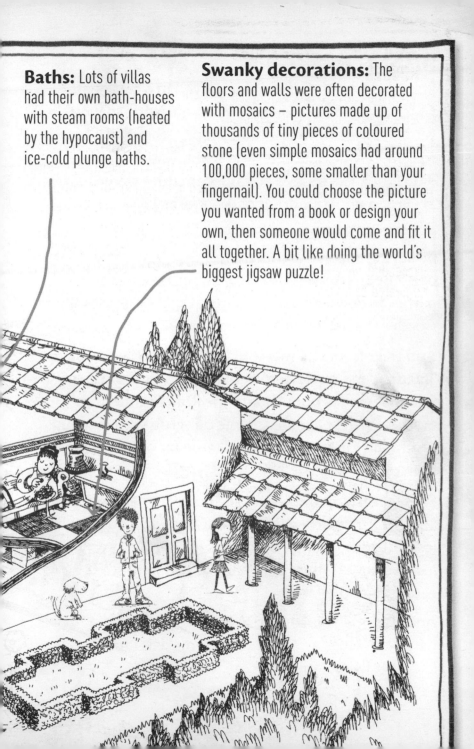

BAKED DORMICE

Romans loved their food. If you lived in a small flat which didn't have a kitchen, your mum or dad would get takeaways from fast food shops – things like bread soaked in wine, sausages, and pizzas (although they didn't look like today's pizzas – tomatoes weren't grown in Europe until hundreds of years later!).

But if you were rich, your mum and dad would show off by having massive dinner parties that lasted hours – one emperor served a meal of 22 courses. At these parties they would eat really extravagant dishes – the weirder the better!

And their favourite was stinky fish sauce. It was called '**garum**', and made of rotten fish guts. Boy, did it smell! But it was really popular and the Romans put it on everything, just like we splurge our grub with ketchup! Garum factories were often located far outside towns – I can't think why!!

For big feasts, cooks would stuff one animal inside another – maybe a chicken stuffed inside a duck stuffed inside a goose stuffed inside a pig stuffed inside a cow! It must have felt like you were eating an entire farm!

And they made joke food too; things like roast hare with wings attached to it, to make it look like a big flying rabbit!

SLAVE KIDS

Slavery was very common in Roman times. If you were rich, you had lots of slaves to do things for you. On the other hand, if you were a foreign child who'd been captured by the Romans, you had to spend your whole life being somebody else's slave . . . great, huh?

Slaves were sold at public auctions in marketplaces – they had to stand with a scroll around their neck which described their name, their nationality, and what they looked like. Slave dealers had to guarantee the slaves they sold were free from disease and wouldn't steal anything or run away. If there was something wrong with them, like they were really sick or they'd tried to commit suicide because they were so lonely, they could be returned and the owners got their money back.

A rich man could own 500 slaves and an Emperor might have more than **20,000!**

Having slaves was great – slaves would . . .

- carry your books to school
- clean your room
- cook your food
- wash your clothes

. . . and they could be made to do this over and over again without you having to pay them any money.

Being a slave wasn't so great. If you were lucky you might work for a nice family who looked after you and gave you decent food to eat. If not you'd be overworked and underfed, and you'd get beaten if you complained about it.

Unskilled slaves were sent to work on big farms, sweating in the fields all day in the hot sun or doing hard, horrible work underground in mines.

PULL!

Roman traders even had slave-powered ships, rowed by slaves who were chained to the oars.

Slaves often had their faces branded with a mark (by burning them with hot metal) or wore collars like dogs so that people would know who they belonged to.

Even if your master died, you weren't freed – you were just passed on to somebody else. The only way to stop being a slave was if you were set free by your master, or if you saved enough money to buy your freedom. This was pretty difficult, though, because slaves weren't paid anything.

FVGITENEME
CVMREVOCV
VERISME·DM
ONINOACCIPIS
SOLIDVM

This collar was found in Rome.

THE SONS OF MARS

PART THREE

While he was in Gaul, Julius Caesar (that moustache-hating army general you met on page 50) led a couple of expeditions across the English Channel to take a look at a strange island known as 'Britannia'.

BLUE BANDY BRITONS

He told the Romans that the Britons wore their hair long and shaved every part of their body except their heads and upper lips – more moustaches! And before battle, they used a natural dye to paint themselves blue, which made them look pretty scary in a fight.

But as they had lots of cattle and precious metals, he thought the Britons were probably worth conquering, although not by him, as he'd got more important things to do.

Like the Gauls, the Britons were divided into lots of different tribes. Some of them wanted to be friends with Rome, but others thought Rome was a very bad thing indeed.

Eventually, in 43 AD, the Romans finally invaded. Some tribes welcomed them with open arms, while others cracked open the blue paint and got busy sharpening their battle swords!

The Romans successfully conquered most of the tribes in the south and east, and Britannia became part of the **Roman Empire**. There was just one problem – there were quite a lot of tribes which still hadn't been beaten, and they weren't going to go down without a fight . . .

BRITISH TRIBES WHEN THE ROMANS ARRIVED

Brigantes

Parisi

Deceangli

Ordivices

Coritani

Iceni

Cornovii

Catevellauni

Demetae

Silures

Dobunni

Trinovantes

Atrebates

Cantiaci

Belgae

Regnenses

Durotriges

Dumnonii

BOUDICCAN REVOLT

One of the tribes which hadn't yet been conquered was called the Iceni (pronounced *I-see-nee*). They'd done a deal with the Romans, which allowed them to remain free as long as they paid 'tribute' (which meant giving Rome lots of presents).

But when their King died in 60 AD, the Roman Emperor said the land of the Iceni must now be handed over to Rome. And if the Iceni didn't like it – tough nuts! So who was going to stand up for the Iceni?

Come on, if you think you're hard enough!

A statue of Boudicca in London. Nice wheels!

The answer was **Boudicca** (pronounced *Boo-dik-ah*), the wife of the former king. She raised an army and marched south to attack the Roman base at Colchester. Other tribes, who also hated Rome, joined in and the revolt spread.

After seizing Colchester, Boudicca's army attacked the new Roman towns of London and St Albans. Today if you dig deep into the ground in these cities you'll find a layer of black and red ash – this is the remains of the buildings Boudicca's army destroyed!

You might be asking – what were the Romans doing while all this was going on? Well, their legions had been busy fighting tribes in Wales – and as soon as they heard what Boudicca was up to, they rushed back.

The two armies finally met on a Roman road called Watling Street. The Romans were outnumbered 10 to 1 and stood facing hundreds of thousands of wild screaming Britons with painted faces – men and women – clashing their weapons, blowing trumpets and thumping drums.

But if you think this made the Romans nervous – think again. This was the Roman army remember . . . and the Roman army knew their way around a battlefield.

Fight! Fight!

HOW TO FIGHT LIKE A TORTOISE

The Roman army was trained to fight in close formation – thousands of soldiers could march forward or back, and turn left or right, without bumping into one another. Each man's shield overlapped the next to make a wall of shields, with the pilums (big sticks) and spears sticking out in front.

One famous formation was the '**testudo**' or 'tortoise'. Men stood in a square with shields round the sides and over their heads to form a protective shell. These shields were so strongly interlinked that it was said you could drive a horse and chariot over the top!

RRAAARGH!!

Another formation was called the '**wedge**'; legionaries formed up in a triangle, then the blokes at the front charged forward, with their swords driving the enemy line apart.

Most importantly, the Roman army always formed up carefully, quickly and in **total** silence! This took incredible discipline and would've been very off-putting for the enemy – it's a bit scary to see that the army you're about to fight is quietly getting ready to obliterate you.

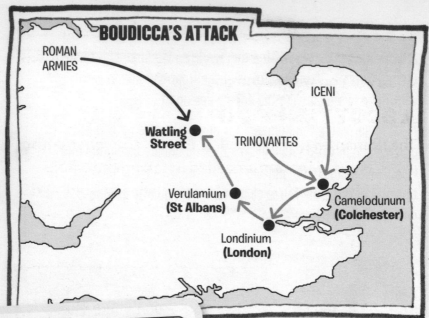

BOUDICCA'S ATTACK

ROMAN ARMIES

Watling Street

ICENI

TRINOVANTES

Verulamium (St Albans)

Camelodunum (Colchester)

Londinium (London)

BATTLE OF WATLING STREET

Date: 61 AD approx.

Roman Army: 10,000

Britons: 100,000+

Score: Romans – 1, Britons – 1 (Rome wins on penalties after extra time)

Wo-Man of the match: Queen Boudicca (10/10 for effort, 1/10 for technique)

Riding in a chariot, Boudicca led her troops in a charge against the Roman legionaries. Unfortunately it was like running into a wall (a wall with sharp spikes sticking out of it). The British tribes retreated in confusion and chaos. The Romans marched on, slaughtering everyone in their path.

By the end, only 400 Romans had died and 80,000 Britons had been killed! It was a massacre (or 'a glorious victory' if you were a Roman).

A SCOTTISH MUG

The Romans went on to defeat a lot of the other British tribes but they never succeeded in taking the whole island. They gave up when they reached Scotland, and built a big stone wall across the whole of northern England to mark the border of the Empire.

It was called 'Hadrian's Wall' because it was built during the rule of the Roman Emperor Hadrian. It took the army eight years to put it up, and it had forts and towers positioned all along it so the army could keep an eye on the barbarians beyond.

CALEDONIA (Scotland)

BRITANNIA (Britain)

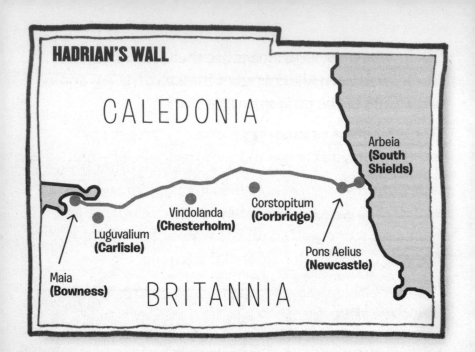

HADRIAN'S WALL

CALEDONIA

Arbeia
(South
Shields)

Luguvalium
(Carlisle)

Vindolanda
(Chesterholm)

Corstopitum
(Corbridge)

Pons Aelius
(Newcastle)

Maia
(Bowness)

BRITANNIA

There are still long unbroken stretches of Hadrian's Wall you can walk along today.

Hadrian's Wall was so impressive that the Romans made souvenir mugs with pictures of the wall on them and the names of the forts round the rim!

The remains of Hadrian's Wall and its forts are still standing, so you can go and see it for yourself – and maybe get your own mug while you're there.

LITTLE BRITONS

One of the forts near Hadrian's Wall was called 'Vindolanda' (look at the map opposite) and in the 1970s a load of Roman wooden writing tablets were found there preserved in an ancient rubbish dump. They include fragments of letters from soldiers stationed on the wall, including birthday invitations and requests for more beer! They tell us that the soldiers called the local tribes 'The Brittunculi' or 'Little Britons' and that they missed the warm weather of home. One letter is a reply to a soldier who'd asked for more underpants!

Vindolanda fort has been recreated for visitors.

THE RISE OF A SLAPHEAD

For a long time, the Roman Republic was really successful – power was shared between the Senate and the people of Rome, and although there were lots of rows and the occasional uprising, by and large it was working out OK. But then things started to go wrong . . .

Meanwhile rich Roman politicians were pocketing bribes and fixing prices to make sure they got even richer.

And then everyone started fighting over how Rome should be run. Things looked bad.

The men perfectly placed to take advantage of this aggravation were the generals of the Roman army – experienced leaders with thousands of men at their command.

And which general reckoned he could rule Rome better than anyone else?

Who'd launched the first expedition to Britannia?

Who'd smashed the hairy Gauls?

Who was a national hero?

Cool it, guys. I'm in charge now!

Hooray!!

Yes, you've guessed . . . **Julius Caesar**.

He marched back home with a legion of soldiers and made himself 'dictator' of Rome.

Being dictator meant that everyone had to do what he said. In the past 'dictators' had been appointed at times of crisis, but only for six months, after which they'd handed control back to the people.

But Caesar had no intention of handing over to somebody else – ever; oh no . . . he made himself dictator for life!

Statues of Caesar dressed like a god were put up and his face was stamped on Roman coins so everyone knew who was in charge. But he was very vain. On the coins he insisted on wearing a crown of leaves round his forehead to cover his big shiny bald head.

Baldy, aka Julius Caesar, wearing his wig.

Caesar won the support of ordinary Romans by spending lots of money on public games and banquets, cancelling debts and doing massive makeovers on the big public buildings in Rome.

Unfortunately for him, he didn't win everybody over. Some people thought he was too powerful. In 44 BC Caesar was assassinated – stabbed on the steps of Senate House. The men who killed him believed they were freeing Rome from tyranny and restoring power to the people – hurrah!

Unfortunately that was utter rubbish. All that happened was another lot of generals started fighting over who should take Caesar's place – boo!

NEVER IGNORE A CHICKEN

Nowadays most people who want to have a chat with their god pop down to their local place of worship and do a bit of praying. But not the Romans. Their religion made them do some seriously crazy things, like sticking their hands in animal guts and looking for hidden messages, chopping the heads off dead bodies, and running around dressed in goat skins whipping people!

Sometimes this was just a way of having a wild time, but mostly they did it because they thought it would keep the gods happy. They had lots and lots of gods, and they didn't want to make any of them angry. It's easy to understand why – the gods were...

THE FAMILY FROM HELL!!!

Mmm . . . tasty.

Saturn was the grand-daddy of the gods. He tried to eat all his children so they wouldn't take over from him.

Jupiter was the son of Saturn – one of the few of his children who managed to avoid being eaten. He fought his dad and became king of the gods. He had a thunderbolt which he threw at anyone he didn't like.

Neptune was Jupiter's brother and the god of the sea. When he was feeling grouchy and bad-tempered he stirred up the ocean and wrecked ships.

Juno was Jupiter's wife, and queen of the gods. She spent a lot of time arguing with her husband, bossing him about or flirting with him to get her way.

Are you, looking for a fight?

Mars was the son of Jupiter, the god of war and the dad of Romulus and Remus. He was a thug who loved nothing more than a good bloody battle. The Romans thought he was great!

Mercury was the son of Jupiter. He could move around really fast and was a thief and a trickster. He tried to steal Jupiter's thunderbolt but burned his fingers!

Venus was the goddess of love and beauty. She was the girlfriend of Mars, but often pranced around without any clothes on and got off with loads of other blokes. She was always poking her nose into other people's love-lives.

TOO NUDE FOR KIDS!

Imagine having that lot living next door!

SPOT THE GOD

The Romans believed the gods were everywhere. Apart from Saturn and Mars and their family, they thought there were gods in the trees, stones, lakes, caves and flowers, as well as in things like stoves and beds. They even thought there was a little god who lived in the latch that opened the door to your house!

So how did the Roman worshippers keep all these squabbling gods happy?

By doing exactly the same thing that makes you and me happy . . . they gave them presents!

Not iPhones and trainers. Usually they handed over things like food, money or flowers. But on special occasions they presented the gods with their favourite present of all . . . the **blood and guts** of a really big animal!

VEGETARIANS SHOULD NOT READ THIS NEXT BIT AS IT'S RATHER DISGUSTING!

GRACE'S NOTES ON HOW THE ROMANS SACRIFICED A BIG ANIMAL

1 They took the biggest and best cow, pig or sheep they could find!

Who me?

2 They scrubbed it up until it looked really cute, and decorated it with pretty ribbons.

3 Then they led it to the temple, and handed it over to the priest.

OINK . . . OOIIINNK!

CENSORED!

4 The priest cut its throat, drained it blood, removed its insides and burned them on an altar.

5 The priest's helpers cooked the animal on a barbecue and served it up to everyone with lots of wine.

Sometimes over a **hundred** animals were sacrificed at one time. This was pretty messy, though, and meant all the worshippers ended up with bursting bellies, grease round their mouths and sticky fingers!

WHAT DOES IT ALL MEAN?

Romans were always looking for signs to tell them whether the gods were happy or angry. These were known as 'omens'. If you saw a bad omen, it meant the gods were upset and the safest thing to do was go home, lock the door and hide under the bed.

Help! It's the end of the world . . .

If a black cat entered your house, it was an awful omen. So was a cock crowing during a banquet. If you spilt wine or oil, or tripped over your doorstep, big trouble was coming.

If I was a Roman I'd never have left my house!

Before anything important was done in Rome – like passing a law or going to war – professional omen-readers were brought in to find out what the gods thought. They looked for omens in lots of things. For instance . . .

The weather: When a storm blew up and thunder and lightning kicked off, they listened to it to try and work out what the gods were saying.

Animal guts: A priest would cut open the belly of an animal to see if there were any signs from the gods in the shape and colour of its guts.

That doesn't look good . . .

Bird song: They watched birds flapping about, and listened to them chirruping, because they believed that the birds were transmitting coded messages from the god Jupiter.

LISTEN TO THAT CHICKEN

The Roman army swore by omens too. They took sacred chickens with them into battle, and before attacking they'd choose one and crumble some food in front of it. If the chicken ate the food, it was a good omen; if it didn't, the omen was most definitely **BAD**.

In 249 BC before a sea battle, a sacred chicken refused to eat and the commander threw it overboard – saying if it couldn't eat, then at least it could drink! Of course, he lost the battle – which proves you should always listen to a sacred chicken!

I'm simply NOT hungry.

A SERIOUSLY BAD OMEN

In the year 114 BC, there was a really bad sign. A sacred priestess at one of the temples in Rome was struck by lightning . . . GASP!

People thought the temple priestesses had seriously annoyed the gods by having boyfriends, which was the worst thing a priestess could do.

There was only one way to make the gods happy again – sacrifice some humans!

So they took two Greeks and two Gauls and buried them alive under the marketplace. Now you probably think that this was not only incredibly cruel, but also incredibly stupid. But the Romans reckoned it worked, because after that not one single priestess was struck by lightning again.

MONSTERS

Ancient Romans also believed in monsters, including:

- **witches** who could change into birds

- men who became **wolves** when it grew dark

- and a serpent-tailed **demon** called 'Lamia' who stalked the shadows looking for children to eat.

It's a wonder anyone could sleep at night.

And if that's not creepy enough, they also believed in ghosts called 'lemures'. They said that if you didn't give dead people a proper burial, they would come back as lemures and haunt you. To stop that from happening, they chopped the heads off the dead, and put heavy stones on their coffins. The lemures can't have been all that creepy, though, because if you had a 'lemures' problem, all you had to do to scare them away was bang your cooking pots!

Don't hit the pots too hard: they're made of clay!

BURIED WITH RUBBISH

The dead weren't allowed to be buried inside the walls of a city, so the roads leading out were always lined with burials. This meant that people who wanted to go to a funeral had to go on a big hike.

The Romans loved a nice funeral. If you died, you were given a good wash and laid on a couch in your nicest clothes for eight days. Then there'd be a big procession. If you weren't very popular your relations would hire some professional mourners who'd make a big fuss over you and make it look like everyone missed you!

Your body was either put straight in a stone tomb or else it was burned on a big bonfire, after which your ashes were tipped into a pot and then placed in the tomb.

Wail, wail, even more wailing . . .

This bunch is blowing trumpets at the dead person . . . just to make sure she's really dead!

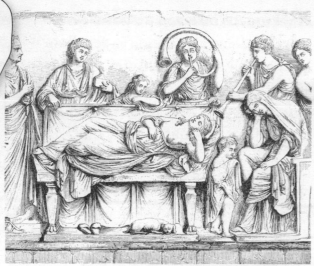

Every Roman wanted a nice funeral; even slaves would put together the few pennies they had saved up to pay for one. They knew that if they couldn't raise the cash, they'd get no funeral at all. Instead their body would be dumped in a pit on the outskirts of town at a grim place called 'Potter's Field', along with the local rubbish, dead animals and the scrapings off the road.

POTTER'S FIELD

The Romans believed that after you died, your soul went to the underworld. To get there it had be rowed across the River of Death on a little ferry, and to make sure the ghostly ferryman did his job properly and didn't lose your body or mess about with it, a coin was placed in your mouth to pay him.

Some Romans believed that the more you paid, the better your journey across the River of Death would be, so they were buried with their jewels, in order that they could travel first class!

Charon the ferryman arrives to take the dead across the River Styx.

Fares, please!

CHRISTIANS FOR LUNCH

Christianity started when the Romans crucified Jesus
Christ in about 30 AD. They thought he was a dangerous
troublemaker who'd disrespected their gods. They
didn't think much of his followers either, because
Christians only believed in one God and refused to
worship any of the others – not even those little ones
living in your door latches.

The Romans believed the Christians were putting Rome in danger by not worshipping Mars (the god of war, remember?) and the rest of his family. They thought the gods would get cross about this and bad things would happen. So they started rounding up the Christians and killing them in all sorts of horrible ways, including feeding them to lions!

Despite this, Christianity spread right across the Empire. People were simply impressed by all these brave Christians who'd rather die than give up their religion!

Early Christians couldn't shout about their faith, so they used a fish symbol (drawn in the dirt or on a wall) to let other believers know they were Christians.

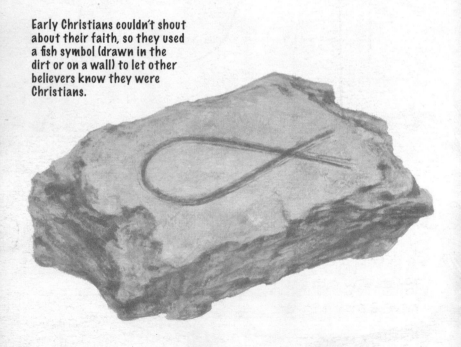

ROME'S CRAZIEST EMPERORS

After Julius Caesar was assassinated there was a long civil war, at the end of which his nephew Octavian became ruler of Rome. He was the first person to call himself 'Emperor', which meant 'Supreme Commander', and he changed his name to Augustus, which meant 'the Great One'. He certainly wasn't shy, was he?

From then on, around 27 BC, Rome was no longer a Republic, it was officially an 'Empire' and it carried on being one for hundreds of years.

There were about 140 Roman Emperors in total. They were the most powerful men in Rome, with oodles of money and an army at their command. If you lived in the Empire you had to do whatever the Emperor said.

When an Emperor died, the new Emperor was often one of his relatives, even if they weren't the best person for the job.

Some Emperors were good, some were bad and some were just plain **crazy** – I'm talking about the most demented, unhinged, half-baked, 'mad as a box of frogs', 'one-way ticket to the loony bin' freaks ever to put on a toga ...

This would have been funny if they hadn't had the power of life and death over everyone in the Roman Empire.

Caligula (reigned 37-41 AD)

Another early Roman Emperor was Caligula. A few months after taking power, he came down with a strange illness, which seems to have turned him into a total nutter. He proclaimed himself a god and built a temple with a life-size gold statue of himself inside it. He raised taxes so he could roll around on piles of gold coins, and held lavish banquets where he drank pearls dissolved in vinegar. He even made his pet horse a senator and built him a big marble stable to live in!

Caligula was a fan of violence and torture – once at a sporting event he ordered the first five rows of the audience to be thrown to the lions because he was bored. His favourite method of torture was hanging people upside down and sawing them in half.

Nero (reigned 54–68 AD)

Nero was a big show-off. He took part in chariot races where he made sure he was crowned the winner even if he lost. He also put on shows where people were forced to sit and listen to him acting and singing for hours and hours. Some of the audience even pretended to be dead so they'd be carried out!

Don't stop me if you've heard this one before.

He thought everyone was plotting against him (which they probably were) so he got rid of anyone he didn't trust – including his own mother. He poisoned her (but she took an antidote), crushed her bed with a collapsible ceiling (but she escaped) and sabotaged a boat so that it would sink when she was on it (she survived and swam ashore). Finally he sent three assassins to stab her to death and then pretended it was suicide. That one worked!

PURPLE PEOPLE

Roman Emperors often wore special purple robes – purple dye was very rare and expensive: only the rich could afford it. It came from a type of sea snail and you had to crush up thousands of them to get even a few drops of dye. The colour became known as 'imperial purple' and it was forbidden for anyone else in Rome to wear that colour. The sale of purple was even punishable by death!

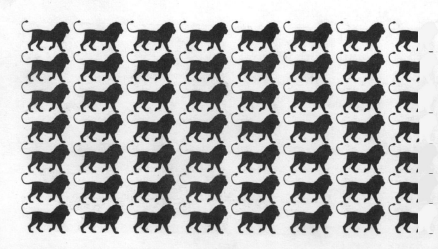

Commodus (reigned 177–192 AD)

The Emperor Commodus loved pretending to be a gladiator (a kind of professional wrestler), although his fights weren't always fair, particularly when he decided to take on people with no arms or legs. In fact sometimes he tied them up beforehand – he wasn't taking any chances, was he? He also loved fighting exotic animals – he boasted that he'd slaughtered 100 lions in a single day, killed three elephants single-handedly and shot the head off an ostrich.

If you were an insane Roman Emperor you had to watch out – there were always people plotting to get rid of you. Even good Emperors often came to a sticky end – knocked off by relatives, politicians or even their own bodyguards! No wonder they were paranoid.

FUN STUFF

If you were a smart Emperor you'd spend loads of money putting on free entertainment for the ordinary people, because this made you really popular!

Plus, if everyone was busy watching sport, they might not notice when you did something really unpopular like raising taxes.

CHARIOT RACING

A Roman writer once said that there were only two things that ordinary Romans were interested in – cheap food and 'circuses'.

He didn't mean circuses with clowns, acrobats and tightrope walkers.

A 'circus' was the Roman name for a stadium that put on chariot races.

Chariot racing was Rome's most popular sport – just like football is today. And the 'Circus Maximus' was Rome's Wembley Stadium. In fact it was bigger! It could hold up to 250,000 people – more than double the number of people who can fit into Wembley – and entry was free!

El Djem in Tunisia held 35,000 spectators for chariot racing or gladiator fights.

Charioteers were divided into teams – the blues, the greens, the whites and the reds – and they all wore their team colours. Fans followed their favourite team and knew all about the different horses and drivers. The best drivers were treated like Premiership footballers – they earned loads of money and had their pictures put on things like cups, sculptures and mosaics.

Some Romans would do anything for their team – at the funeral of one Red driver, a Red supporter threw himself on the funeral bonfire along with the body ... and you thought football fans were crazy!

The Romans were so obsessed with chariot racing, they even put pictures of it on their coins.

At the start of each race, the chariots lined up in front of gates. When they were all ready, a cloth was dropped on the floor to signal the start. The gates sprang open and the teams of horses thundered on to the track.

On your marks, get set, giddy up!

Chariots were usually pulled by four horses, and the driver would wrap the reins around him to help steer. Competitors would deliberately try to make their opponents crash. If a chariot turned over, the driver was dragged around the track and often trampled to death.

Not surprisingly, a chariot driver wasn't expected to live long – one celebrity driver called Scorpus won over 2,000 races before being killed in a crash when he was only twenty-seven years old.

GLADIATORS

The only thing more dangerous than being a charioteer was being a gladiator – a trained fighter who risked his life in front of sell-out crowds.

The Colosseum in Rome was a massive four-storey stone arena with tiered seats for 50,000 spectators. The word 'arena' means 'sandy place' because the floor was covered in sand to soak up all the blood. And the best seats were at the front, close to the action. If you were lucky you might even get splatted with gore!

The remains of the Colosseum are still standing in Rome today.

Lots of different shows were put on at the Colosseum – animal fights, hunts, public executions and battle re-enactments – but the most popular were the gladiator fights. Men, women and children flocked to watch these contests . . . it was a fun day out for all the family.

The name 'gladiator' comes from the Roman word 'gladius' or sword. Armed with swords, spears and daggers, they fought each other or ferocious wild animals like lions and tigers (who'd often been starved for days so they were extra hungry and grouchy). It was often a fight to the death – the winner was the last man (or lion) left alive.

Roman animal collectors went all round the Empire gathering up exotic beasts to put in their gladiator shows – leopards, lions, tigers, elephants and bears. So many were killed that whole species almost became extinct!

The gladiators had as little choice as the animals – most were slaves, criminals or prisoners-of-war taken

The bloke in the big hat isn't trying to look up the skirt of the one with the giant fork. He's stabbing him in the leg.

captive and forced to become gladiators. If they refused to fight they were executed. If they were good enough, they might win fame and fortune – and eventually maybe even their freedom.

Some free men also signed up because of the glory and the prize money . . . and because they were nutters.

They trained at special 'gladiator schools' where they practised fighting with different weapons. Gladiators were difficult to replace, so while they were alive they were well looked after, with lots of food to eat and doctors on hand to treat their injuries.

JOJO'S FAVOURITE GLADIATORS

I'm really hard.

Retiarii ('net fighters') – carried a trident, a dagger and a net to entangle their opponents.

Sagittarii ('archers') – mounted on horses and armed with a bow and arrow.

Thraces ('Thracian soldiers') – armed with a small shield, a wide-brimmed hclmct and a curved sword.

Andabatae (horseback fighters) – dressed in chainmail, wore helmets without eyeholes (!) and charged blindly around the arena.

Essedarii (war charioteers) – named after the chariots the Celts rode into battle.

I'm the hardest!

Bestiarii (animal fighters) – armed with spears or knives, they fought exotic imported beasts.

But it wasn't just fully grown men who fought. There are descriptions of women and dwarf gladiators.

The fights were part of spectacular shows with music, props and scenery (just like going to the theatre but with more severed limbs). Under the floor of the Colosseum were underground chambers and tunnels. Slaves pulling on ropes could hoist scenery or animals up through trapdoors into the centre of the arena. If you wanted to stage a sea battle, the whole place could even be flooded with water from the nearby aqueduct!

Gladiator fights often had referees. They were probably needed to make sure the fight was fair and to call half-time – even ferocious gladiators needed a bit of a rest now and again.

Once a gladiator had floored his opponent, it was up to the crowd (or the Emperor if he was watching) to decide whether the loser was to be killed or spared. Sometimes if both men had fought well, they were both allowed to live to fight another day.

Crowds showed they wanted the loser to die by with a 'pollice verso' – Latin for 'turned thumb'. But did that mean thumbs up, or down? No one knows!

SPARTACUS

Some Romans worried about the use of gladiators. They thought putting lots of slaves, criminals and ex-soldiers together, teaching them how to kill and giving them weapons might lead to trouble. And guess what . . . they were right!

In 73 BC, seventy gladiators led by an ex-soldier called Spartacus, broke out of a Gladiator School in southern Italy, seizing weapons and armour on the way out. They raided the surrounding countryside and recruited other slaves to join their revolt.

They knew it wouldn't be long before the army would be sent to sort them out, so they made their way up to the top of the volcano Mount Vesuvius. This wasn't such a daft idea as it sounds: the volcano was dormant – meaning it was safe to climb – and from the top they could see anyone coming to get them.

We demand our freedom – and some trousers.

Three thousand Roman soldiers were sent to deal with the gladiators. They camped out at the bottom of the volcano and waited for them to starve. But Spartacus and his men weaved ropes out of vines and abseiled down the cliffs on the other side, then launched a surprise attack on the camp, killing the soldiers and stealing their kit.

It was clearly going to take a whole lot more to stop Spartacus – so next Rome sent two whole legions (10,000 strong) to wipe out the slaves. But even that wasn't enough to stop them! By now lots of slaves across Italy had heard what was going on and joined the revolt – Spartacus soon had a force of over 70,000 men!!

Now people back in Rome got really panicky – there were a lot of slaves in Rome: what if they all started rising up? Who'd be left to do all the rubbish jobs like scraping dead skin off the floor of the baths or washing togas in vats of urine?

This time, eight legions were sent to put down the revolt and the slave army was finally destroyed.

We don't know what happened to Spartacus – he might have been killed in battle, or maybe he was one of 6,000 defeated slaves crucified afterwards along the Appian Way – the main road into Rome.

Rome wanted to make it very, very clear to every slave that they mustn't ever do anything like that ever again. Do you have a funny feeling that the Romans were getting a bit scared?

THE EMPIRE FALLS APART

At first Emperors tended to survive for quite a long while, even if they were barking mad like Nero and Caligula, but people got fed up with all this scary behaviour and tried to put a stop to it. Soon Emperors were lucky if they lasted more than a couple of years before getting poisoned, stabbed, having their heads chopped off, being pushed down the stairs or suffocating to death with their own underpants (OK, as far as I know, no Roman Emperor was actually suffocated to death with his own underpants ... but I'm sure somebody thought about doing it).

Some Emperors only lasted a few weeks before they were bumped off!

But while everyone in Rome was busy scheming and plotting and knocking off Emperors ... the Empire was falling apart.

WATCH YOUR BACK

Often Emperors ended up being killed by the men paid to protect them ... their own bodyguards!

The Praetorian Guard was a unit of elite soldiers whose job was to look after the Emperor and keep order in the city of Rome – a bit like a police force.

But if you paid them enough money they might switch sides and assassinate the Emperor for you ... handy. Sometimes they got fed up with the Emperor and, just for the fun of it, killed him and replaced him with somebody else.

Once they even held an auction and sold the job of Emperor to the highest bidder!

I think I should have stayed at home.

When Emperor Galbus didn't pay the Praetorian Guards, they rioted ... and killed him!

TOO BIG FOR ITS BOOTS

The land the Romans ruled over was now absolutely ginormous – it had swollen from a tiny bunch of villages to an Empire bigger than even cocky Romulus could ever have dreamed of – 2.2 million square miles, to be precise, with a whopping 120 million people living in it.

Lots of the places you might visit on holiday – like France, Spain, Italy, Germany, Greece, Turkey and Egypt – were all once part of the Roman Empire. The Romans built towns in all these places and the people who lived there started calling themselves 'Romans', speaking Latin and wearing trendy togas.

ALL ROADS LEAD TO ROME

To help people get round their colossal Empire, what did the Romans build? Well, if you know nothing else at all about the Romans, you probably know that they built roads . . . lots of them . . . over 53,000 miles of them . . . by hand! . . . and most of them were dead straight!

So you're probably thinking: roads aren't anything special. They're just big, dark grey things that graze my knee when I fall off my bike. But in the past if you wanted to get anywhere you had to trudge along little winding tracks, sinking up to your knees in mud whenever it rained. Now everyone could travel in style along wide stone roads that linked up all the places in the Empire.

Roman roads were made as straight as possible to make the journey quicker but they weren't always **totally** straight – the Romans weren't stupid: if there was a big mountain in the way, they went around it!

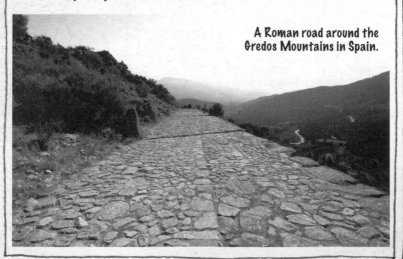

A Roman road around the Gredos Mountains in Spain.

The Appian Way in Rome. This was one of the first important Roman roads ever built. When it was finished, it connected Rome in the north to Brindisi all the way down in the south, 350 miles away.

A PROBLEM HALVED

The trouble was, as the Empire got bigger and bigger, it got harder and harder to run – there just weren't enough soldiers or money to keep it all going. In fact it got so bloomin' massive no one could hold it together.

In 284 AD the Emperor Diocletian tried to make things easier by cutting the Empire in two – a Western Empire and an Eastern Empire, each with its own ruler.

Unfortunately, it would have taken more than a pair of scissors to solve all Rome's problems.

A DIVIDED EMPIRE

How do you divide the Roman Empire?

Use a pair of Caesars!

Eastern Empire

Western Empire

I'M BORED!

Slaves did all the work in ancient Rome. They slaved away in factories and down mines, they cleaned toilets, washed clothes and cooked food, Educated slaves worked as teachers, librarians, artists and even doctors! One in four people in the city of Rome was a slave!

At first, having loads of slaves to do all your work for you seemed like a great thing – nobody else had to lift a finger. Instead you could spend all day pottering around the shops, gossiping to your mates about the latest chariot race or how long it would be before someone suffocated the Emperor with his own underpants.

But having so many slaves turned out to be a bad thing for Rome. People got lazy. Some rich Romans relied so much on their slaves that they couldn't even remember how to dress themselves!

More importantly, lots of poor Romans couldn't get work because the slaves did everything! Without a job, people couldn't afford food and had nothing to do all day. The government had to spend lots of money giving out free grub and putting on gladiator fights to keep everyone amused!

Because this was very expensive, the Emperors kept raising taxes – which made everyone even poorer and very fed up.

RAMPAGING BARBARIANS

As if that wasn't enough to worry about, the Romans also had to deal with hordes of barbarians on the rampage!

Peewee's Notes on How to Spot a Barbarian

The Huns – a fierce bunch of armoured horsemen all the way from Mongolia (near China), led by the legendary 'Attila the Hun'. They rode across Europe, raiding towns, burning and plundering pretty much everything in their path. Everyone was terrified of them: it was said that they drank the blood of their captives and tied the severed heads of their enemies to their saddles.

Grrr . . .

If you treat us like dogs, we'll bite!

The Goths – (not the kind you see in the city centre today who wear black clothes, big boots and dark eyeliner). These were tribes living on the northern borders of the Roman Empire, who moved to Rome to get away from the horrible Huns. Unfortunately, the Romans weren't very welcoming (refusing to give them any land and only giving them dog meat to eat!). So the Goths got stroppy and took a load of land for themselves.

The Vandals – The Vandals were another tribe who moved into the Empire to escape the Huns. They set up home in North Africa and used ships to sail across the Mediterranean and launch attacks on Roman coastal towns. When the Romans tried to stop them, the Vandals won a sea battle by setting fire to some ships and sailing them into the Roman fleet!

We vandalized those Romans.

The Anglo-Saxons – The Roman army left Britain in 410 AD because Rome needed all its soldiers back home to fight the barbarians. This left the door wide open for the Anglo-Saxons – a group of tribes from across the North Sea. They took over, and it's from them that we get the name 'England' (Angle-land).

These tribes and others like them all moved into the Empire and started setting up their own little kingdoms. There wasn't much the Romans could do about it – their army was big but it wasn't that big: it couldn't fight them all!

Not even the city of Rome was safe – in 410 AD it was invaded by an army of Goths ... **the first time in 800 years that the city had been attacked!** Thousands of Roman citizens fled to the countryside and many of its grand buildings were trashed.

There are thousands of Roman ruins all over Europe. This is Palmyra in Syria.

ROME? NEVER HEARD OF IT

Eventually, half the Roman Empire collapsed.

The tribes who took over in the West didn't want to speak Latin or wear togas – they had their own languages and their own way of doing things.

Villas, aqueducts and roads fell into ruin, libraries were destroyed and lots of people forgot how to read and write. The Fall of Rome was so traumatic that the centuries after it happened are sometimes called the 'Dark Ages' because of how much was lost.

WE'RE STILL HERE!

But it wasn't all doom and gloom. For a start, the Roman Empire in the East survived!

The capital of the Eastern Empire was Constantinople (now Istanbul in Turkey) and was named after the Emperor who built it – the Emperor **Constantine**.

LOOKING CROSS

In 312 AD, Constantine was about to go into battle when he looked at the sun and saw a cross of light and the words '**If you use this sign, you'll be a winner!**' So he ordered his troops to paint crosses on their shields, and sure enough he won the battle.

Constantine was in York (Eboracum) when he was proclaimed Emperor. His statue is outside York Cathedral.

NO MORE HUMAN SNACKS

Emperor Constantine isn't just famous for building a big city in Turkey. He was also the first Christian Roman Emperor.

The last time I mentioned the Christians they were being fed to lions. But how things change . . .

Understandably, Constantine became a big fan of Christianity. He stopped the persecution of Christians (no more being thrown to lions – hurrah!) and built lots of shiny new churches everywhere.

Constantine even put Jesus on the coins.

By the end of the fourth century, Christianity was the official religion of the Roman Empire and if you worshipped the old gods you were in big trouble (just like the Christians used to be!).

Constantinople became the 'new Rome'. Huge columns, great chunks of marble and beautiful statues were carted across the Empire and used to build the city.

And just in case any nasty barbarians were lurking nearby, the Romans put up enormous walls round it to protect it from attack.

Constantinople became the centre of the Eastern Empire. It was full of palaces, public baths, Roman ideas and Roman inventions – and it lasted another thousand years. **Romulus's dream was still alive.**

Istanbul today is still full of Roman buildings.

Me too!

ROMANS TIMELINE

3000 BC   Early hieroglyphs are invented

753 BC   Rome starts off as a farming village

509 BC   Rome becomes a republic

221–210 BC   In China, the First Emperor of the Qin Dynasty is building up his own empire

216 BC   Hannibal thrashes the Romans at the Battle of Cannae

200 BC   The Romans first use concrete

79 BC   Pompeii is destroyed when Mount Vesuvius erupts

73 BC   Spartacus breaks out of gladiator school to lead a slave rebellion

52 BC   The Gauls are beaten inside AND out at the Siege of Alesia

44 BC   Julius Caesar is assassinated

27 BC	Rome becomes an Empire, and Octavian is the first person to get the job of Roman Emperor
30 AD	Jesus Christ is crucified by the Romans
37–41 AD	Caligula is Roman Emperor
43 AD	The Romans invade Britain
54–68 AD	Emperor 'Show-Off' Nero is in charge
61 AD	Boudicca clashes with the Romans at the Battle of Watling Street
177–192 AD	Emperor Commodus rules (and kills plenty of lions)
284 AD	Emperor Diocletian chops the Empire into two bits, West and East
312 AD	Emperor Constantine 'sees the light' and becomes a Christian
410 AD	The Roman army gets out of Britain
410 AD	An army of Goths attacks Rome
406–453 AD	Life of Attila the Hun

ROMANS QUIZ

1 Which Carthaginian crazy trekked over the Alps to attack Rome?

2 What did the Romans build to take water from one place to another?

3 What was the Roman version of loo roll?

4 Where's a great place for a business meeting with an ancient Roman?

5 How long did Roman soldiers sign up for?

6 What did Roman schoolkids use instead of paper?

7 What was the Romans' favourite stinky fish sauce called?

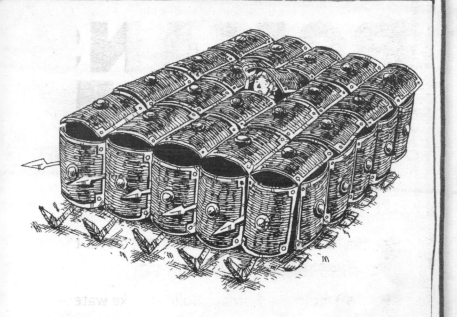

8 What did Roman soldiers shout as they formed a tortoise shape?

9 Which sacred bird should you look after if you want to win a battle?

10 Which colour of clothes was illegal for anyone but the Emperor to wear?

Picture Credits

left to right
t = top; b = bottom; r = right; l = left; c = centre

Shutterstock images: 3 A_Belov; 6 Andrei Nekrassov; 12 marcello mura; 22 Croato; 27t katad; 27b Jiri Pavlik; 29 edo; 33 Anibal Trejo; 35t Matthew Collingwood; 35b Justin Black; 37 Bill Perry; 39 meunierd; 42 HENX; 43 Kevin H. Knuth; 55 Elnur; 59 Kate Connes; 60 Pete Kilmek; 65 Offscreen; 68 F.C.G.; 80 Vladimir Korostyshevskiy; 86 Ian MacDonald; 87 Jaime Pharr; 90 Kamira; 90 Aquila; 91 Andrei Nekrassov; 96 javarman; 97 Vladimir Korostyshevskiy; 103 Ross Ellet; 105 riekephotos; 108c Kenneth V. Pilon; 113 alessandro0770; 114 PLRANG; 115 Lagui; 119 Gelia; 121 Faraways; 122 majeczka; 123 Olga Matseyko; 124 Clara; 125 nito; 129 Teerapun; 130 pseudolongino; 136 Brian Maudsley; 137 imagestalk; 144 WitR; 146 imagestalk; 147t Simon Smith; 147b Kenneth V. Pilon; 148 Vitaly Titov & Maria Sidelnikova and Eon Images: 92, 107, 111 and 133; KF Archive 28, 111 and 116r; Loicwood 15; Marie-Lan Nguyen/Wikimedia Commons 116l.

Also available in this series

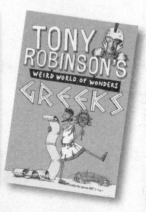